MARK TWAIN'S

YOUTHFUL ADVENTURES

US AUTHOR WITH THE WILDEST IMAGINATION

**Biography 6th Grade
Children's Biographies**

DISSECTED LIVES
auto biographies

First Edition, 2020

Published in the United States by Speedy Publishing LLC, 40 E Main Street, Newark, Delaware 19711 USA.

© 2020 Dissected Lives Books, an imprint of Speedy Publishing LLC

Dissected Lives Books are available at special discounts when purchased in bulk for industrial and sales-promotional use. For details contact our Special Sales Team at Speedy Publishing LLC, 40 E Main Street, Newark, Delaware 19711 USA. Telephone (888) 248-4521 Fax: (210) 519-4043. www.speedybookstore.com

10 9 8 7 6 * 5 4 3 2 1

Print Edition: 9781541950924
Digital Edition: 9781541952720

See the world in pictures. Build your knowledge in style.
www.speedypublishing.com

TABLE OF CONTENTS

Birth and Early Life 5

From Riverboat Pilot to Writer 13

Livy's Influence on Twain 28

Mark Twain's Books 43

The Adventures of Tom Sawyer 47

The Adventures of Huckleberry Finn 58

SUMMARY 68

In this book, we're going to talk about the life of famous American author Mark Twain, so let's get right to it!

BIRTH AND EARLY LIFE

Mark Twain, whose real name was Samuel Langhorne Clemens, was born in November of 1835 in a tiny village called Florida in the state of Missouri.

Mark Twain's birthplace, Florida, Missouri

When Samuel was only four years old, his father took their family to another city in Missouri called Hannibal, which was located close to the mighty Mississippi River.

Mark Twain in front of his boyhood home in Hannibal Missouri

Here, Samuel grew up and experienced many of the adventures that later appeared in numerous forms in his novels. His happy boyhood was filled with days along the riverbanks.

HANNIBAL, MISSOURI.

HANNIBAL IN MISSOURI.

In a memoir of his life, published in 1883, he detailed the thrill and excitement of the townspeople when the languid summer days were interrupted by a cry of "The Steamboat's Coming."

Mississippi Steamboat, 1883

All of a sudden, in practically the blink of an eye or the toot of a horn, the sleepy town would wake up as everyone waited for the beautiful boat to come down the river.

Townsfolk from Hannibal marvel at the steamboat

These events made an indelible impression on young Samuel. In fact, his pen name, Mark Twain, comes from the riverboat term for calling out that water was twelve feet or two fathoms deep—"Mark Twain."

A tourist steamboat in Hannibal, Missouri. The "Mark Twain."

The riverboat town of Hannibal was Mark Twain's true home and the relatives who lived there and the friends he made remained in his memory forever and became the inspiration for the spirited characters in his books.

The town of Hannibal, Missouri

FROM RIVERBOAT PILOT TO WRITER

Before any of his books were written, Twain needed to see more of the world and develop some wisdom. When he was just seventeen years old, he left his beloved hometown to find work in print shops as a printer's assistant. He secured these jobs in New York as well as Pennsylvania and Iowa.

Young Samuel Clemens (A.K.A Mark Twain) holding a printer's composing stick

Then, four years later, he came back to the Mississippi River where he would train for the position he wanted most in the world—a job as a pilot of a steamboat.

Statue of "Mark Twain - Steamboat Pilot", Riverfront at Hannibal

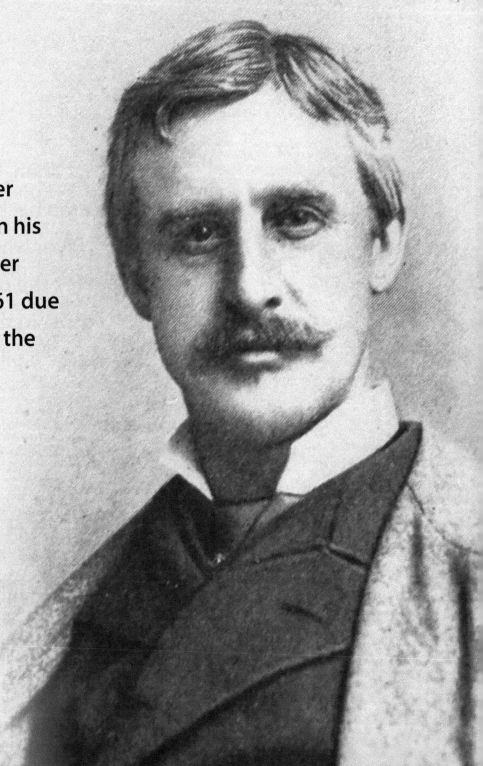

He worked hard over several years to gain his license, but his career was cut short in 1861 due to the beginning of the Civil War.

Mark Twain, 1861

He fought as a Confederate soldier for a few weeks before he decided to head out west.

American Civil War, 1861

His brother was living in Carson City, Nevada and once Twain joined him he began to try his hand at writing for the local paper. He started by writing funny articles and tall tales and it was in February of 1863 when he began to publish his work under the pen name, Mark Twain. Eventually, this pseudonym would be known around the world.

MARK TWAIN

100 YEARS AGO, IN 1864, SAMUEL CLEMENS LEFT THE TERRITORIAL ENTERPRISE, MOVING ON TO CALIFORNIA AND WORLD-WIDE FAME. HE WAS A REPORTER HERE IN 1863 WHEN HE FIRST USED THE NAME, MARK TWAIN. HE LATER DESCRIBED HIS COLORFUL ADVENTURES IN NEVADA IN "ROUGHING IT."

NEVADA CENTENNIAL MARKER NO. 27

PLACED BY

JAMES LENHOFF, 1964

EDITOR AND PUBLISHER
TERRITORIAL ENTERPRISE

But, he wasn't making a living yet from writing, so he took a job as a miner not too far from San Francisco at the end of the era called the Gold Rush.

The Gold Rush in California

During this time, while working in the minefields, he heard a tall tale that he later wrote as a short story, "The Celebrated Jumping Frog of Calaveras County." When it was published in 1865, it became an overnight success and was printed and reprinted many times.

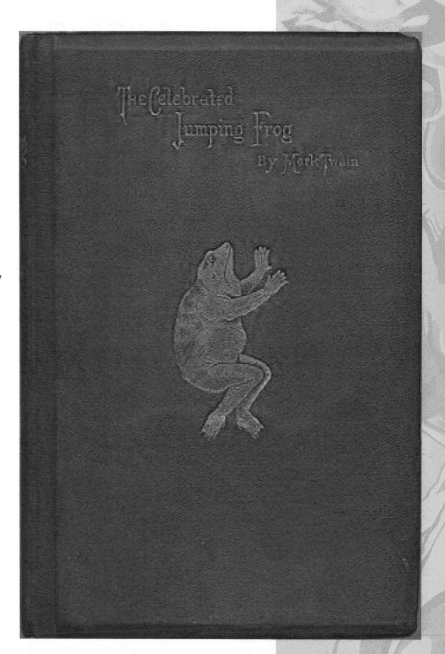

1st Edition of The Celebrated Jumping Frog

COOPER INSTITUTE

The Sandwich Islands.

By Invitation of a large number of prominent Californians and Citizens of New York,

MARK TWAIN

WILL DELIVER A

Serio-Humorous Lecture

ENTITLED

KANAKADOM

OR,

THE SANDWICH ISLANDS,

AT

COOPER INSTITUTE,

On Monday Evening, May 6, 1867.

TICKETS FIFTY CENTS.

For Sale at Chickering's Store, 652 Broadway, and at the Cooper Institute.

Doors open at 7 o'clock. The lecture will begin at 8.

Twain was itching to see the world so he set out for the Sandwich Islands, now called Hawaii, and began to write travel pieces for various publications.

Mark Twain poster for Sandwich Islands or Kanakadom talk May 6, 1867 at the Cooper Institute, New York

In 1867, he left for a trip to Europe and to the Middle East on the Quaker City, a steamship. On the long voyage, he became friends with Charles Langdon.

Mark Twain and Charles J. Langdon

Charles showed Twain a photograph of his sister Olivia, nicknamed Livy for short. Twain fell in love at first sight and wanted to meet Livy when they were back in the United States.

Olivia Langdon

Eventually, Twain put all his travelogues together to create a book called *The Innocents Abroad.*

Book cover of Innocents Abroad by Mark Twain

LIVY'S INFLUENCE ON TWAIN

Livy Langdon and Samuel Clemens were a case of opposites attracting. She came from a proper, well-to-do Eastern family and Samuel, now known as Mark Twain, was a rugged, wild Westerner. She was a pious, religious, educated young woman and he was a man who had grown up poor. He was self-educated and he was prone to smoking, drinking, and sometimes swearing.

Livy Langdon and Samuel Clemens

When he went to Elmira, New York to visit her and her family, she turned him away as a suitor and refused his proposal of marriage.

Map of New York State

However, she decided that what he needed was to be reformed so she agreed to write letters to him. For the next 17 months, he wrote her a series of more than 150 letters professing his love for her.

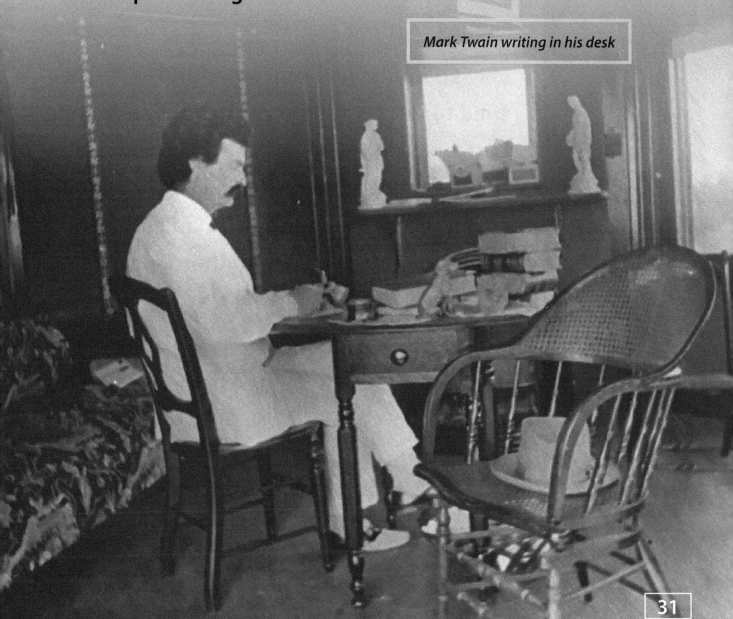

Mark Twain writing in his desk

Livy's parents were concerned and when they tried to ask for references from their friends in the West, they found out that Samuel was quite wild. However, the fact that he had confessed his ways honestly had earned him points and helped Livy's father take a liking to him.

Mark Twain, 1867

Twain convinced Livy to marry him. They became engaged in 1869 and married a year later.

Mark Twain with wife Olivia

Livy's father showered love and wealth upon the couple. He bought them a home in the city of Buffalo, New York and supplied them with servants.

Mark Twain and Livy's home in Buffalo New York

He even gave Twain a loan to buy ownership of a newspaper. Soon, Twain's novel *The Innocent Abroad* was published and he quickly gained both fame and a considerable fortune.

THE VILLAINOUS DONKEYS. 419

get down and lift his rear around until his head pointed in the right direction, or take him under your arm and carry him to a part of the road which he could not get out of without climbing. The sun flamed down as hot as a furnace, and neck-scarfs, veils and umbrellas seemed hardly any protection; they served only to make the long procession look more than ever fantastic—for be it known the ladies were all riding astride because they could not stay on the shapeless saddles

DRIFTING TO STARBOARD.

sidewise, the men were perspiring and out of temper, their feet were banging against the rocks, the donkeys were caper-ing in every direction but the right one and being belabored with clubs for it, and every now and then a broad umbrella would suddenly go down out of the cavalcade, announcing to all that one more pilgrim had bitten the dust. It was a wilder picture than those solitudes had seen for many a day. No donkeys ever existed that were as hard to navigate as these, I think, or that had so many vile, exasperating instincts. Occa-

72 A PRIVATE FROLIC IN AFRICA.

At this present moment, half a dozen of us are taking a private pleasure excursion of our own devising. We form rather more than half the list of white passengers on board a small steamer bound for the venerable Moorish town of Tan-gier, Africa. Nothing could be more absolutely certain than that we are enjoying ourselves. One can not do other-wise who speeds over these sparkling waters, and breathes the soft atmosphere of this sunny land. Care can not assail us here. We are out of its jurisdiction.

We even steamed recklessly by the frowning fortress of Malabat, (a stronghold of the Emperor of Morocco,) without

GARRISON AT MALABAT.

twinge of fear. The whole garrison turned out under arms, and assumed a threatening attitude—yet still we did not fear. The entire garrison marched and counter-marched, within the rampart, in full view—yet notwithstand-ing even this, we never flinched.

44   THE MOCK TRIAL.

No. 10. A judge was appointed; also clerks, a crier of the court, constables, sheriffs; counsel for the State and for the defendant; witnesses were subpœnaed, and a jury empaneled after much challenging. The witnesses were stupid, and unreliable and contradictory, as witnesses always are. The counsel were eloquent, argumentative and vindictively abusive of each other, as was characteristic and proper. The case was

MOCK TRIAL.

at last submitted, and duly finished by the judge with an absurd decision and a ridiculous sentence.

The acting of charades was tried, on several evenings, by the young gentlemen and ladies, in the cabins, and proved the most distinguished success of all the amusement experiments.

An attempt was made to organize a debating club, but it was a failure. There was no oratorical talent in the ship.

We all enjoyed ourselves—I think I can safely say that, but

148   "AMERICAN DRINKS COMPOUNDED."

sign to this effect: "ALL MANNER OF AMERICAN DRINKS ARTISTICALLY PREPARED HERE." We procured the services of a gentleman experienced in the nomenclature of the American bar, and moved upon the works of one of these impostors. A bowing, aproned Frenchman skipped forward and said:

"Que voulez les messieurs?" I do not know what Que voulez les messieurs means, but such was his remark.

Our General said, "We will take a whisky-straight."

[A stare from the Frenchman.]

AMERICAN DRINKS.

"Well, if you don't know what that is, give us a champagne cock-tail."

[A stare and a shrug.]

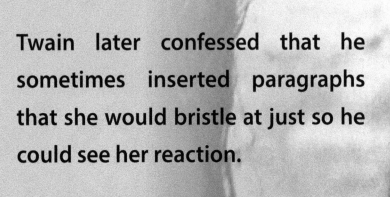

Twain later confessed that he sometimes inserted paragraphs that she would bristle at just so he could see her reaction.

Mark Twain with his family on the porch of his house at Hartford, Connecticut

Twain doted on his wife for she had had poor health as a teenager, which affected her for the rest of her life. He remained deeply in love with her until she passed away in 1904. He never recovered from losing her.

Samuel and Olivia Clemens, 1903, the year before Olivia died

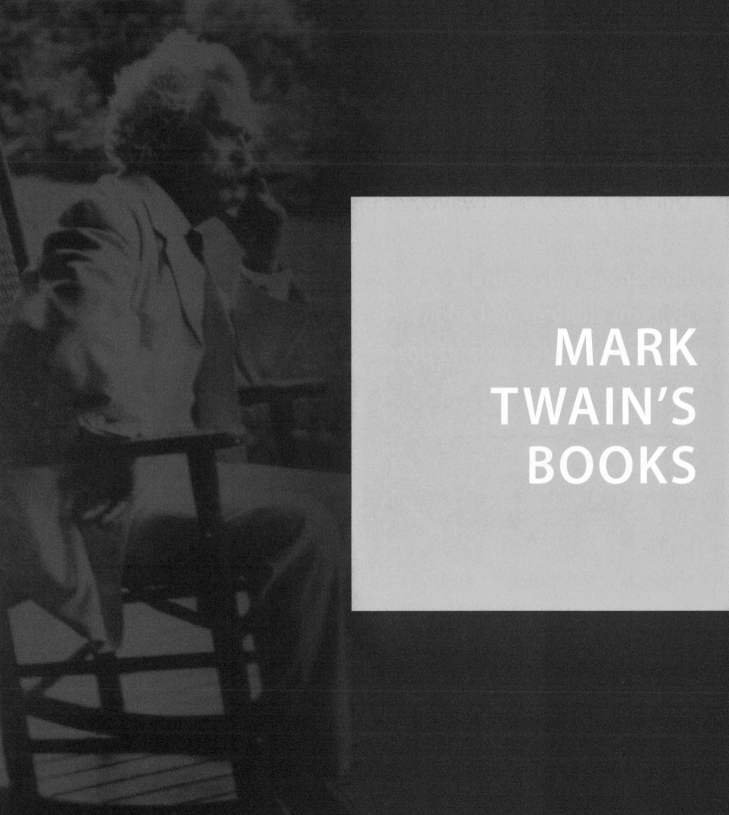

MARK TWAIN'S BOOKS

During his career, Twain became famous around the world for his humorous, adventure books, loved by both children and adults. He wrote more than 25 novels and dozens of short stories.

Mark Twain pondering at his desk

Two of his most famous books, *The Adventures of Tom Sawyer,* which was published in 1876, and *The Adventures of Huckleberry Finn,* which was published in 1884, were based largely on his childhood memories.

 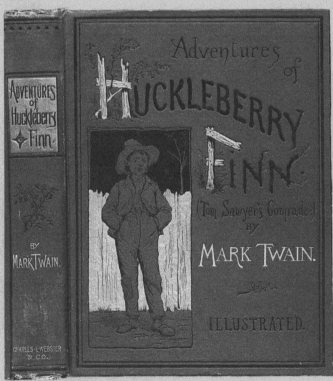

The Adventures of Tom Sawyer **and** *The Adventures of Huckleberry Finn book covers*

He was also known for his lecture tours, where he told funny stories and read passages from his books.

An illustration of "Mark Twain," America's best humorist, circa 1885

THE ADVENTURES OF TOM SAWYER

In 1876, it was America's 100-year anniversary of independence from Great Britain. The United States had grown from thirteen colonies to a booming, expansive industrial country. People began to long for simpler times.

Opening day ceremonies at the Centennial Exhibition at Philadelphia, May 10, 1876

Twain also felt this longing. In the early part of the 1870s, he went back to his hometown of Hannibal and it brought back many of his childhood memories. It inspired him to write *The Adventures of Tom Sawyer*.

Mississippi River from Riverview Park
Hannibal, Missouri

Many parts of the novel highlight the idyllic river life that he experienced in Hannibal, which in his novel was renamed as St. Petersburg after Saint Peter who guards the gates of heaven.

However, the town also had very marked social classes, alcoholics, homeless people, and slaves. St. Petersburg wasn't a perfect heaven. The children and adults in Twain's novel are in conflict with one another.

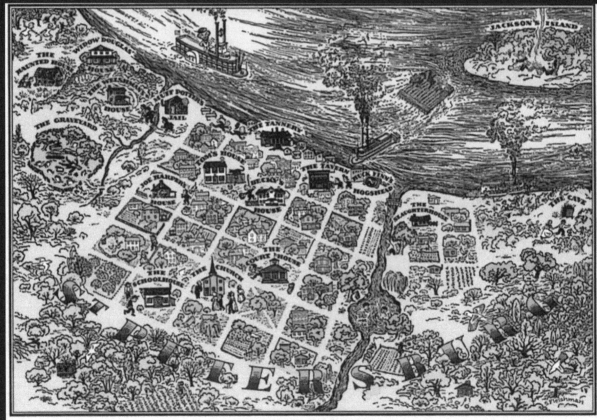

HANNIBAL, MISSOURI
The "St. Petersburg" of Mark Twain's "Adventures of Tom Sawyer"

The "St. Petersburg" of Mark Twain's "Adventure of Tom Sawyer"

Tom and his cohorts appear to run the town behind the scenes. At that time in the US, many children's books showed young boys who were perfect in every way. They obeyed their parents, saved their money, and never ever played hooky from their classes.

An illustration from the book The Adventures of Tom Sawyer

Twain didn't care for these preachy books. He wanted to show young boys in the way he had been as a boy, full of vim and mischief. His main character, Tom Sawyer, is a boy who has an amazing imagination.

Tom Sawyer and his friends swimming in the river

AFTER THE BATTLE.

An illustration of Tom Sawyer and
his friends' adventure

This strength leads him to wealth, close friendships, and adventure. Tom sees the wonder in everyday things and it lifts his spirit higher than the everyday citizens of St. Petersburg.

The book has a serious side, but it is also filled with enduring humor and social commentary. Throughout the book, Twain pointed out the evils of greed, dishonesty, and hypocrisy. Twain was one of the first authors to write everyday dialect speech in his books.

An illustration of Tom escaping from his Aunt Polly

THE
ADVENTURES OF
HUCKLEBERRY
FINN

When *The Adventures of Huckleberry Finn* **was published in 1885, Twain had already garnered fame as an author and humorist. This second "boy's book" was in a way a continuation of the Tom Sawyer story.**

Flyer for Adventures of Huckleberry Finn

Mark Twain's Latest Book.
The ADVENTURES of
HUCKLEBERRY FINN,
Tom Sawyer's Comrade.

EVERY LINE FRESH AND NEW.

NOT a sentence of this book has ever before appeared in print in any form.
All the illustrations are New, and were made expressly for this book at great expense.

WRITTEN IN MARK TWAIN'S OLD STYLE.

This book is simply irresistible, and is pronounced by an author of WORLD-WIDE reputation and HIGH AUTHORITY, who has read the manuscript: "The brightest and most humorous book that Mark Twain has ever written,

A BOOK FOR THE YOUNG AND THE OLD, THE RICH AND THE POOR,

A CURE FOR MELANCHOLY.—Nine-tenths of our ills are due to an over-burdened mind, an over-taxed brain, or imaginary troubles that never come. An amusing book is a panacea more agreeable than medicine and less expensive than doctors' bills.

A MINE OF HUMOR.

Full of startling incidents and hair-breadth escapes, 366 PAGES and 174 ORIGINAL ILLUSTRATIONS, NEARLY ONE HUNDRED PAGES LARGER than "ADVENTURES OF TOM SAWYER," with fourteen more illustrations, better printed, and more attractively bound, yet offered at the SAME PRICE. This book also contains a full-paged heliotype of the bust of the author by Karl Gerhardt, with fac-simile autograph.

☞ HARD FACTS. ☜

Five Hundred and Twenty-five Thousand (over Half a Million) Copies of Mark Twain's Books have been sold in this Country alone, to say nothing of THE IMMENSE SALES IN ENGLAND, GERMANY AND OTHER PARTS OF THE WORLD.

MARK TWAIN'S BOOKS ARE THE QUICKEST SELLING IN THE WORLD.

IN RETURNING TO HIS OLD STYLE OF WRITING, Mark Twain is certainly in his element; for this book, while INTENSELY interesting as a narrative—holding the reader's attention with a tenacity that admits of no economy in the midnight oil—is also at the top of the list as a humorous work. Interwoven in its text are side-splitting stories, sly hints at different weaknesses of society, and adventures of the most humorous description.

All of its FORTY-THREE CHAPTERS are SIMPLY OVERFLOWING WITH INTEREST & HUMOR

In the abstract, the book is the story of adventures of Huckleberry Finn, Tom Sawyer and a negro named Jim, who in their travels fall in with two tramps engaged in TAKING IN the different country towns through which they pass, by means of the missionary dodge, the temperance crusade, or under any pretext that offers to EASILY raise a dishonest dollar.

The writer follows these characters through their various adventures, until we find the tramps properly and warmly clothed—WITH A COAT OF TAR AND FEATHERS—and the boys and Jim escape their persecutors and return safely to their friends.

THIS BOOK IS A COMPANION TO "THE ADVENTURES OF TOM SAWYER," but is complete in itself. No possessor of a Mark Twain book should be without this last and best of his works.

Parties wishing "The Adventures of Tom Sawyer," "The Prince and the Pauper," or any other of Mark Twain's books, can procure them of the agent. No MONEY IS REQUIRED UNTIL THE DELIVERY OF THE BOOK, and no obligation rests with any subscriber to take the book unless it equals in every respect the description given in our circular and the sample shown. The book is now ready and a preliminary canvass proves that it will be the most popular and successful of all of Twain's books. The Richest, Wittiest and Funniest. One agent reports 16 orders in half a day and 90 in six days. Another, that the "very name" sells the book without further effort than the mere offering of the prospectus for signatures. Send for canvassing outfit at once and secure good territory.

SOLD ONLY BY SUBSCRIPTION.

Price in Fine Cloth Binding, Plain Edges,	\$3.50
Leather Library Style, Sprinkled Edges,	4.00
Half Morocco, Marbled Edges,	5.50

SEE THE BOOK. IT SPEAKS FOR ITSELF.

FOR AN AGENCY ADDRESS IMMEDIATELY

THE OCCIDENTAL PUBLISHING COMPANY,
NO. 120 SUTTER STREET,   SAN FRANCISCO, CAL.

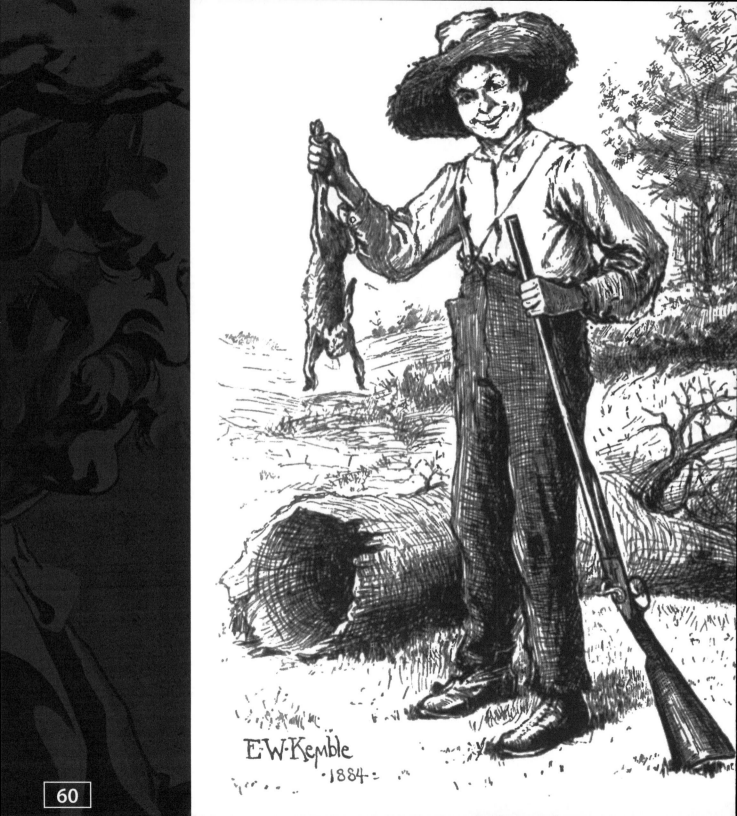

E.W.Kemble
·1884·

Although Huck was ignorant, and poor at the start, he had a good heart. Because Huck was one of Tom's friends, readers expected another series of fun, childhood adventures to be included in this second book.

An illustration of Huckleberry Finn

But, Twain had something more planned for this novel. He had a serious lesson that he wanted to impart. During his adventures, Huck meets Jim, a runaway African-American slave.

Huck meets Jim

At the start, Huck treats Jim just like others treat slaves but as they journey along the great Mississippi River together, Huck's character changes and he realizes the evil inherent in enslaving others. The two end up forming a close, life-saving friendship.

Huck and Jim became close friends

Along the way they meet liars and hypocrites. The novel shows that an individual can overcome society's evils by learning his own personal values through his own experiences and his own heart.

An illustration of Huck and Jim's journey

Even though *The Adventures of Huckleberry Finn* **centers** around important adult themes, it is filled with imaginative misadventures, funny incidences, and odd characters.

Huck and Jim on the raft

Twain tells his story of how a young boy comes of age with humor and heart and with a mastery of the language his characters spoke.

An illustration of Huck lifting a chicken

SUMMARY

Called the father of American literature, Mark Twain was a pen name for Samuel Langhorne Clemens. Twain became a celebrated American author, humorist, and lecturer. He became known around the world for his novels and short stories based upon his childhood life on the banks of the Mississippi River. His work continues to influence writers and delight readers around the world. Two of his most famous novels are *The Adventures of Tom Sawyer* and *The Adventures of Huckleberry Finn.*

Awesome! Now that you've learned about Mark Twain, you may want to read about another famous American, the inventor Thomas Edison in the Baby Professor Book, *Thomas Edison and His 1093 Patents - Biography Book Series for Kids | Children's Biography Books.*

Visit

www.speedypublishing.com

to download Free Baby Professor eBooks and view our

catalog of new and exciting Children's Books

9 781541 976922